A WINNING SKILLS BOOK

You Can Get Organized!

Joy Berry

Illustrated by Bartholomew

Joy Berry Enterprises

Copyright © Joy Berry, 2022
Originally Published 2013

All rights are reserved.

No part of this book can be duplicated or used without the prior written permission of the copyright owner, except for the use of brief quotations from the book.

For inquiries or permission requests contact the publisher.

Published by Joy Berry Enterprises
www.joyberryenterprises.com

You can get organized by learning
- the difference between organized and disorganized,
- how to organize your possessions,
- how to organize your space, and
- how to organize your time.

INTRODUCTION

INTRODUCTION 5

You are **organized** when the space in which you function is neat and orderly. You are also **organized** when your possessions are where they belong.

THE DIFFERENCE BETWEEN BEING ORGANIZED AND DISORGANIZED   7

You are **organized** when you are doing the right things in the right place at the right time.

THE DIFFERENCE BETWEEN BEING ORGANIZED AND DISORGANIZED

You are **disorganized** when your belongings are out of place.

You are disorganized when the space in which you function is messy and disorderly.

THE DIFFERENCE BETWEEN BEING ORGANIZED AND DISORGANIZED 9

You are **disorganized** when you are doing the wrong things in the wrong place at the wrong time.

10 ■■■ THE DIFFERENCE BETWEEN BEING ORGANIZED AND DISORGANIZED ■■■

Being disorganized can cause you to become confused and frustrated. It can keep you from doing the things you need and want to do.

If you are disorganized, you can cause the people around you to become confused and frustrated. Their confusion and frustration might cause them to become angry at you.

THE DIFFERENCE BETWEEN BEING ORGANIZED AND DISORGANIZED

Being organized can make life simpler and more pleasant for you and the people around you.

THE DIFFERENCE BETWEEN BEING ORGANIZED AND DISORGANIZED ■ 13

To be organized, you must efficiently manage your
- possessions,
- space, and
- time.

To organize your possessions, you need to follow six steps.

Step One: Get four large boxes and label them.

Label the first box "Toss."

Label the second box "Recycle."

Label the third box "Hold."

Label the fourth box "Use."

ORGANIZING YOUR POSSESSIONS — 15

Step Two: Put your possessions in a pile.

Step Three: Sort your possessions into the four boxes.

Pick up one possession at a time and put it in one of the four boxes. Do not put the item back in the pile.

All of the possessions that are no longer useful should be put in the box marked "Toss."

ORGANIZING YOUR POSSESSIONS 17

Usable possessions you do not want any more should be put in the box marked "Recycle."

ORGANIZING YOUR POSSESSIONS

When you have not used something for a long time and are not sure you want to get rid of it, put it in the box marked "Hold."

All the possessions you want to keep and use should be put in the box marked "Use."

Step Four: Distribute the four boxes.

Put the contents form the box marked "Toss" in the trash.

Get rid of the possessions in the "Recycle" box. The items in this box can be
- given to a friend,
- traded for something else,
- sold, or
- given to an organization that recycles used things.

Close up the "Hold" box. Write the date on it. Then store the box in a safe place.

If a year goes by and you have not missed the possessions in your "Hold" box, you probably don't need them. In this case, put the unwanted items in the "Recycle" box next time you organize your possessions.

Step Five: Sort the possessions in the box marked "Use."

The items in this box can most likely be divided into these groups.

1. Reading material (such as books, magazines, and comic books)
2. School materials (such as notebooks and homework)
3. Arts and crafts materials
4. Stationery supplies (such as paper, pencils, and erasers)
5. Hobbies (such as model airplanes and miniatures)
6. Collections (such as stamps, rocks, and baseball cards)
7. Toys and games
8. Equipment (for sports, bikes, etc.)
9. Music and musical instruments
10. Clothing (including shoes and boots)
11. Personal supplies (such as combs, brushes, and perfume)
12. Mementos (such as photographs, scrapbooks, and keepsakes)

Step Six: Put away the items from the "Use" box.

- Put anything smaller than a Ping-Pong ball into plastic storage bags. This includes items such as game parts, accessories, and model pieces.
- Place items the same size of a baseball in shoeboxes or covered cans.
- Store all the items in one group together in a box if there is no room in drawers or closets.
- Label your possessions so they can be returned to you if they are misplaced.
- Label drawers, shelves, and boxes so anyone who puts away your things will put them in the right place.
- Get rid of worn-out or outgrown things before you put away any new ones so you won't gave to dig through the pile of old things to get to the new ones.

Here are a few tips for organizing your clothes:
- Group you clothes according to a plan. You might want to put all your shirts or blouses together, all you pants together, and so on. Or you might want to put your play clothes together and your good clothes together. Any plan you decide to use should help you find things more easily.
- Put freshly laundered clothes on the bottom of the stacks of folded clothes in your drawers and on your closet shelves. Use the clothes on top first. If you do this, everything will be worn, and you won't end up wearing the same clothing over and over.

ORGANIZING YOUR POSSESSIONS

It will be easier for you to organize your possessions if you **work in a clean area.**

It will also help if you work with **one group of possessions at a time.**

ORGANIZING YOUR SPACE

Your space includes the areas you live in and use. At home it might be your bedroom and bathroom. At school it might be your desk or locker. To organize your space, you need to follow four rules.

Rule One: Every item in your space should have a purpose.

Every item in your space should have a reason for being there. Get rid of items that do not have a purpose. Useless items take valuable space and make it difficult to keep the area organized.

Rule Two: Every item in your space should be used properly.

You should use every item in the way it was intended to be used. For example, a clothes hamper, rather than a chair, should be used to collect dirty clothes. A trash can, rather than a drawer, should be used to collect trash. Beds should be used for resting, not for hiding junk. Rugs should be used to cover the floor, not to cover dirt.

ORGANIZING YOUR SPACE

Rule Three: Every item in your space should be assigned to a specific place.

Every item in your space should have a certain place where it can be stored. If there is not a specific place for something, you need to create a place for it. To do this, you can

- get rid of something you do not use,
- use boxes or other containers for storage, or
- make a shelf by stacking a board on some cinder blocks or bricks.

Rule Four: Every item in your space should be in it's place when it is not used.

When you have finished using something, you should carefully put it back in its place. If you do this, your possessions will not become damaged and your space will look neat and orderly.

ORGANIZING YOUR SPACE

It will be easier for you to put things away if you store them properly.

Things used often should be put in places that are not easy to reach.

Things used occasionally can be stored in places that are not so easy to reach.

ORGANIZING YOUR TIME

To organize the time you spend doing various activities during the day, you need to follow four steps.

Step One: Gather together the necessary equipment and supplies.

You will need
- a clock (preferably an alarm clock),
- a watch (optional),
- a wall or desk calendar (with space in which to write),
- a date book,
- a note pad, and
- a sharpened pencil

Here's what to do:
- Put the clock in a place where you can easily see and use it. If you have a watch, wear it.
- Hang the calendar or put it in a place where you can easily see it and use it..
- Carry the date book with you or keep it at school.
- Keep the note pad by your calendar.
- Keep a sharpened pencil by the calendar and note pad.

Step Two: Gather together dates and information.

Go to the office at your school. Get the dates for
- school vacations,
- school holidays, and
- school events.

ORGANIZING YOUR TIME

If you belong to a team, club, or organization, talk to the people in charge. Get the information for
- regular meetings (such as practices and weekly get-togethers) and
- special meetings (such as games and parties).

Be sure to get the date, time and location of each event.

Talk to your parents or guardians. Get the information for
- family vacations,
- family holidays, and
- family activities (such as parties and outings).

Be sure to get the date, time, and location of each event.

Write the information you have gathered on your calendar and in your date book. Write the name, time, and location of each event next to its scheduled date.

Use a pencil when you write so you can erase the information if your plans change. This will help you avoid making a mess of your calendar or your date book.

ORGANIZING YOUR TIME

Step Three: maintain your calendar.

When someone asks you to do something, check your calendar or date book. Look at the date and time he or she has asked you about. If nothing is written for that time, you can think about doing what the person has asked you to do.

If you decide to do what someone has asked you to do, write the information about the event on your calendar and in your date book.

Check your calendar at the beginning of each day to remind yourself of activities planned for the day. Mark off each day or event on your calendar after it occurs.

Step Four: Maintain a things-to-do list.

Anytime you think of something that needs to be done, write it on the note pad next to your calendar. If you are not near your note pad, write a message about the task on a scrap of paper. Put the message in your pocket or purse. When you get to your note pad, transfer the message from the scrap of paper to the note pad. Be sure to check your pockets or purse for your messages at the end of each day.

Check your note pad at the beginning of each day. Decide when and how you are going to do tasks listed on the note pad. As much as possible do what you have decided to do during the day.

At the end of every day, check your note pad. Cross off the things you have done.

Put the things you have not done at the top of your list for the next day.

There are two sayings that might help you as you go over your things-to-do list.

First saying: "First things first."

You need to do the most important things on your list first. The other things should be done in order of their importance.

Second saying: "One step at a time."

You might feel overwhelmed if you try to do everything at the same time. When you have a lot of things to do, you need to do them one at a time.

CONCLUSION

Life is easier and more pleasant for you and the people around you when you organize your
- possessions,
- space, and
- time

www.ingramcontent.com/pod-product-compliance
Lightning Source LLC
Chambersburg PA
CBHW081408070526
44583CB00020B/2730